26

#26
Angeles Mesa Branch Library
2700 W. 52nd Street
Los Angeles, CA 90043

 W9-AVT-452

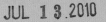
Pebble® Plus

Look Inside

Look Inside a Castle

by Jenny Moss

Consulting Editor: Gail Saunders-Smith, PhD

Consultant: James Masschaele
Professor of Medieval History
Rutgers University

CAPSTONE PRESS
a capstone imprint

Pebble Plus is published by Capstone Press,
151 Good Counsel Drive, P.O. Box 669, Mankato, Minnesota 56002.
www.capstonepress.com

092009
005618CGS10

Books published by Capstone Press are manufactured with paper
containing at least 10 percent post-consumer waste.

Library of Congress Cataloging-in-Publication Data
Moss, Jenny, 1958–
     Look inside a castle / by Jenny Moss.
     p. cm. — (Pebble plus. Look inside)
     Includes bibliographical references and index.
     Summary: "Simple text and photographs present castles, including their construction, history, and interaction with
the environment" — Provided by publisher.
     ISBN 978-1-4296-3985-9 (library binding)
     1. Castles — Juvenile literature. 2. Civilization, Medieval — Juvenile literature. I. Title. II. Series.
GT3550.M68 2010
940.1 — dc22   2009023391

Editorial Credits

Gillia Olson, editor; Kyle Grenz, designer; Wanda Winch, media researcher; Eric Manske, production specialist

Photo Credits

Alamy/architecture UK, 15
The Art Archive/Real biblioteca de lo Escorial/Gianni Dagli Orti, 5
Art Life Images/Alberto Paredes, 21
The Bridgeman Art Library International/©Look and Learn/Private Collection/men digging moat around castle, English
     School, (20th century), 13; The Stapleton Collection/Private Collection/Ancient Kitchen, Windsor Castle, engraved
     by William James Bennett (1787–1844) from 'The History of the Royal Residences' by William Henry Pyne
     (1769–1843) pub. 1818, 17
Chantier médiéval de Guédelon/C. Duchemin, 9, 11
Shutterstock/Cliff Lloyd, 1, 22–23; Condor 36, back cover, 3; Sean Gladwell, 7; ultimathule, cover
SuperStock, Inc./age fotostock, 19

Note to Parents and Teachers

The Look Inside series supports national social studies standards related to people, places,
and culture. This book describes and illustrates castles. The images support early readers in
understanding the text. The repetition of words and phrases helps early readers learn new
words. This book also introduces early readers to subject-specific vocabulary words, which are
defined in the Glossary section. Early readers may need assistance to read some words and to
use the Table of Contents, Glossary, Read More, Internet Sites, and Index sections of the book.

Table of Contents

What Is a Castle?

A castle is a stone building.

Walls often surround castles.

Kings and nobles lived

in these strong buildings.

Castles kept them safe.

4

Castles were built in Europe
in the Middle Ages.
They were common
after the year 1000.

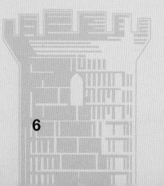

Building a Castle

Building a castle often took

up to 10 years.

Hundreds or even thousands

of men worked

on just one castle.

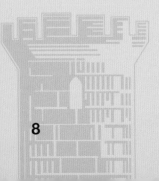

9

Masons stacked stone blocks

to build the outside walls.

Within the walls, they built

a stone tower called a keep.

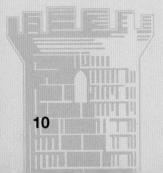

Workers dug a moat

outside of the walls.

They filled the moat with water.

A wooden drawbridge

was lowered to cross the moat.

Inside a Castle

The largest room in the castle

was the great hall.

The king or other nobles

met visitors and

threw parties there.

15

Stone walls and floors could

be cold and damp.

People used rugs and

tapestries to warm up

their bedrooms.

Castles Today

Today, people tour castles.
Visitors learn about life
in the Middle Ages.

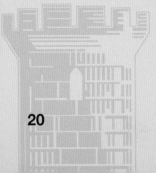

Glossary

drawbridge — a bridge that can be raised up and let down

keep — the strongest part of a castle, usually shaped like a tower

mason — someone who builds or works with stone, cement, or bricks

Middle Ages — the period of European history between about AD 476 and 1500

moat — a deep, wide ditch dug all around a castle and filled with water to prevent attacks

noble — a person of high rank or birth

tapestry — a heavy piece of cloth with pictures or patterns woven into it

tour — to take a trip on a set route, often for sightseeing

Read More

Morley, Jacqueline. *You Wouldn't Want to Live in a Medieval Castle!: A Home You'd Rather Not Inhabit.* New York: Franklin Watts, 2008.

Rau, Dana Meachen. *Castle.* The Inside Story. New York: Marshall Cavendish Benchmark, 2007.

Whiting, Jim. *Medieval Castles.* The Middle Ages. Mankato, Minn.: Capstone Press, 2009.

Internet Sites

FactHound offers a safe, fun way to find Internet sites related to this book. All of the sites on FactHound have been researched by our staff.

Here's all you do:

Visit *www.facthound.com*

FactHound will fetch the best sites for you!

Index

Word Count: 167

Grade: 1

Early-Intervention Level: 18